So You Want to be a Druid?

First steps on the path

By Gladys Dinnacombe

ISBN: 978-1-291-49372-6

Also by Gladys Dinnacombe

Poetry and Prose

Sacred Journey - Sacred Earth

Preface

Since I have let people know that I am a druid, I have been asked a lot of questions about druidry and how could people learn about it in a practical and easy way. This book is the result. Each chapter is a lesson with practical work and often several short meditative journeys. The reader is encouraged to keep a journal; a large notebook in which they can write down their experiences, draw or add photos. It will be a record of their journey into druidry.

Lesson 1

So you want to be a druid?

Do you know what a druid is or what a druid does?

Well, this is a practical guide so get your notebook out and write down what you think a druid is and what a druid does.

Now, I'll tell you about my druidry. I love nature, the planet and all things on our planet. I believe that everything is interconnected and I honour and respect all things on our planet. That will do to start with.

So let's do some real practical work. I want you to find a space outside, a garden, a patch of land with trees or flowers, or a park. Make sure you have your notebook with you, pen and pencil, a blanket if it is chilly and a camera if you have one. Find a comfortable place to sit. If it is chilly, wrap your blanket around you to keep you warm.

Now just sit for a minute or two, then slowly start to look around you. Write down what you see; for example, trees in full leaf, birds, squirrels, moving clouds in the sky. This is a lesson in observation so now spend more time looking at each item in turn. Describe the trees or draw a sketch or take a photo. Do the same with all the other things you see.

Now close your eyes and listen for several minutes. Try to ignore or shut out any traffic noise and tune in with the sounds of nature. When you feel you have heard all you need to hear, then open your eyes and write in your notebook about everything you heard.

Then close your eyes again, but this time try to sense what is going on around you. Is there a breeze ruffling your hair or caressing your face? Do birds flying past move the air around you? What about your feet? If they are planted on the ground then you may feel the energy of the earth moving into your feet. This part of the exercise may take several sessions of practice before you sense this. Again, write in your notebook everything that you sensed.

I did this exercise a few months ago while sitting in the local town park. Here are my notes:

'Sitting in the park on a wooden bench which feels warm in the sun. The river is behind me, lots of reflections from the overhanging trees and bushes. A few birds sitting in the trees, possibly sparrows. The trees are in full summer bloom, leaves bright and moving gently in the breeze. The river is rippling gently over small rocks, sometimes diverging around a larger rock. The sun is shining, making the ripples on the water shimmer. There are a few white puffy clouds in the sky.

I hear the rippling of the water; it is not a steady drone but a gentle change of pitch, quite a musical sound. I can hear some birds chirping, one bird, possibly a blackbird, singing and another bird making warning sounds. If I listen carefully I can hear the gentle rustle of the leaves.
I feel the breeze against my face and I notice when it changes direction. I sense the energy of the earth through

my feet and I allow this energy to move through my body. It brings with it a deep feeling of peace and of being at one with nature and the world.'

If you took photographs with a digital camera then you can view them on your computer. Choose three or four that give a good impression of the area in which you did the exercise and print them out. You can prop or pin them where you can see them every day for a few days. Keep looking at them and compare what you see in the photos with your notes. Did you miss anything? After a few days you can paste the photos into your notebook so you have a full record of that exercise.

You have done your first lesson in observation, learning how to be aware of nature around you. Now it is time to repeat the exercise but in a different place and with different weather. If your first session was in sunshine, choose a cloudy day for the next one. This second session should be easier as you are now more aware of how to 'see' what is going on around you and also what kind of sounds to listen for. The sensing part may take some time before you feel any results so don't worry about it.

Here are a few words I wrote in my blog a while ago. I think they show us what we miss when we are not aware.

'We all seem to have busy lives and we rush from one place to another so that we can do all the things we think we have to do. But we miss so much. I watched a mother hurry her child across the footbridge over the local stream because she wanted to get home quickly. The child wanted to see if there were ducks or fish in the stream, but did not get the chance to stop and look. If we don't give our children the chance to observe nature, how can we expect them to respect it later on in their lives?

The bridge over the stream is a short cut for children going to and from school and people going to work or to the shops. In the last year I have only seen two parents stop and let their children look at the stream. One mother brought her child especially to feed the ducks.

I often stop and watch when crossing the bridge. I have seen the stream in full flood with muddy swirling water rushing past, almost as high as the bridge. One side of the bridge looks upstream to a tiny waterfall. The other side, the stream goes between tall buildings close to the edge of the banks. But here there are buddleias and a small elder tree. There are lots of little inlets where ducks can hide and lots of large stones which can hide various larva, such as that of the caddis fly. I saw a kingfisher earlier this year and my son saw one last weekend. I remember standing still to watch the kingfisher and it seemed that he was very aware of me. When I blinked, he moved and was gone. How did he know when to go?

There are plenty of tiny fish in the stream and when you 'tune' in to the water you can see them clearly. It can be a magical place despite the buildings and the factory car park, but there is no access down to the stream. Perhaps this is a good thing as it prevents human damage to the unique habitats within the stream. '

Here is a photograph of the stream which has been grey-scaled for this book.

So how was your second visit to your chosen area? Your notebook should be filling quite nicely now. This kind of work can be done throughout the year, becoming a long-term project.

You could choose four different places to visit, visiting each in turn once a month. This way you will build up a picture of the area around you and become more observant each time you visit.

You will also build up a connection with these places too. If you have a park near you then try to find the time to explore it.

I am lucky in that we have a town park with lots of mature trees, bushes and shrubs and a river running through the park. It is place where many people walk, some to work, others just to enjoy the park.

The more you visit places of nature, the more you enjoy them and become aware of their special beauty in all seasons and weathers. Look for the hidden life in the fallen leaves, the base of shrubs and trees and on the bark of the trees. You will be amazed at what you see and you will learn to see how things are intertwined and interdependent. Hopefully you will also feel a sense of peace and healing around you and perhaps feel that your energy has been restored.

Lesson 2

The Elements

The elements are an important part of druidry as well as many other spiritual paths. The four elements of Air, Fire, Water and Earth also correspond to the directions of East, South, West and North.

If you look back to your notes on the observation exercises, you will see that Air and Earth are two of the elements that you will have observed. If you were near a river or pond then you will have observed the Water element. We now need to take this further, looking at each of the elements in turn.

Let's look at the element of Air first. In your notebook try to write down at least ten facts you know about air, more if you can. Use the internet or books if you are stuck.

The main fact about Air is that without it we could not breathe. So how do we access the air around us? We feel refreshing breezes; we see clear skies at night, which awaken our perception of what is in our universe and bring in a new awareness. Have you ever stood on the top of a hill when the wind is blowing, or walked against a strong wind or been by the sea when it is stormy? If so, write down how you felt at that time.

I remember my mother saying on a very windy day, 'That will blow the cobwebs away!' She did not mean this just literally but also that it would clear the air, especially that around the buildings and that around our bodies. It is nature's way of cleansing not only stagnant air around buildings but also the energy field around our bodies.

The spiritual conception of air is a much deeper thing.

Air is the element that allows us to communicate with all the inspirational dimensions of our Self. It relates to the transformation of our intelligence, and powers our flights of fantasy into other realms.

Air also allows us the luxury of being able to think before we speak, before we act and gives us the joy of our personal inspiration and creativity.

So how can we work with this element?

If we meditate on this element it will bring new awareness and appreciation, a new view of older images; it helps create new communication skills and invigorates; it brings creative flow and allows us to amplify our thoughts.

Here is an exercise for you:

Practise deep breathing, inhaling to the count of four and slowly exhaling. Do this several times. How do you feel now?

And a few more short exercises. Remember to write down your thoughts afterwards. You could also sketch any images you see.

Visualise yourself with wings, flying in the sky. How does it feel and what do you see beneath you?

Watch how the breeze lifts up things like leaves and litter,
then moves them around. Describe how the leaves or litter
move.

Now for a longer exercise which is more of a meditative
journey. Make sure you are sitting comfortably and will not be
disturbed.

Imagine that you are walking along a snow-covered path
on a frosty morning during the winter. The snow is
sparkling clean and forms a smooth white carpet across
the land. The air seems filled with energy on this bright
morning. Every breath you take fills you with anticipation
and inspiration.

The sparkling snow seems to penetrate your being and
you feel so alive and creative and so full of joy.

You stay for some time, then rush home with a renewed
energy for any projects you have begun. You feel more
resolved about any creative ideas you have had in the
past and determine to bring them to fruition.

A further little exercise that you can do every day is to stand
outside with your eyes closed and take deep breaths. Notice
how the air around you feels. Is it hot or cold? Still or moving?

We can now move on to the element of Earth as this is another
element that you have experienced through your observation
work in Lesson 1.

Let's start again with some facts. Try to find at least ten facts
about our planet Earth then try to find ten facts about the earth

in your garden.

One thing you may have realised is that the Earth has several 'meanings'. We call our planet Earth, then we have the earth in the garden, which mainly consists of soil, and we also often think of our earth as the landscape around us.

If we think about the land around us, we can see that it sustains us, supporting us with the crops we grow and sheltering us with its trees, but it also gives us a connection to our ancestors, those who lived before us and who have left us their stories and their history.

On a spiritual level, Earth helps us to regain our connection to the natural spiritual wisdom and teaches us about ancient tribes and their rituals of power. Earth will sustain us as long as we do not strain its material limitations. (This is the real element of recycling.)

There is something special about walking around our landscape, the feeling of lightness when walking on grass as opposed to walking on stony roads, and a feeling of fulfilment as you tread gently on the earth.

Working in a garden, or even just potting indoor plants, gives a feeling of peace and renewed energy as you see the rewards of your toil. There is also a feeling of connection with the earth as we do this.

So now you can work through some very simple exercises, writing about your experiences in your notebook.

Take a walk on a grassy area, barefoot if possible. Compare the feeling of the earth against your bare feet with the feeling when you are wearing shoes. Write your responses in your notebook.

Lie on the grass letting as much of your body as possible rest on the ground. Close your eyes and listen not just to the sounds around you but to the sounds you can hear going on in the earth beneath you. Now write in your notebook about your experiences.

Work in your garden if you have one. If you don't have a garden then purchase some compost, a few pots and some seeds – herbs are good for this kind of planting. Place them on your windowsill and watch the seedlings grow, nurturing them and loving them too. You can even talk to them if you wish. Note the date when the shoots appear and when the leaves first appear.

Now it is time for a longer exercise, a meditative journey with the element of Earth.

Imagine walking along the top of a moor. The path is quite wide and you can see the landscape around you for many miles. There are wooded valleys and rocky outcrops.

Ahead of you, just off the path, is a large group of rocks close together. You feel drawn towards them, so you pick your way carefully across the springy ground, moving closer to the nearest rock. It glistens and you stretch out your hand to touch it. It feels warm and you decide to lean against it. It is a comforting rock and you close your eyes for a few moments.

When you open your eyes, you move around the rocks until you see a narrow opening. You squeeze through the opening and find yourself in a circular space, open to the sky. In the centre of the space is a smaller rock, just the right size to be used as a seat. You go over and sit on it. It is just the right shape for you and so comfortable that you close your eyes again.

You sense movement around you and whispers. Have the ancients returned here to talk to you? You listen to the sounds and sense everything around you. There is a feeling of peace and of healing and you allow the messages of the ancients to sink into your unconscious mind.

After a while, you realise that it is time to go. You stand up and stretch, looking round for the last time. Just before you enter the opening to the moorland you stop, turn, and say, 'Thank you.' Once you are through the gap and on the open moor again, you find somewhere to sit, get out your notebook and write down all you experienced.

By this time you should be feeling quite connected to the elements of Air and Earth and also be able to see how they connect with each other.

So let's turn to the element of Water now. It should be easy to write down ten facts about water so that is your first task. Do it now.

Water is another element that we need in order to live. We can live without food but not without water, so it is extremely important to us and to all living beings on the planet.

I always feel a sense of awe when I see how everything is interconnected. For example, just as we need water, so do plants and other animals. Water helps to produce our food from crops and it helps the trees and bushes to grow, which provide food for us and small animals, as well as providing shelter.
For now, let's continue to consider the element of Water. Water is cleansing and soothing. After a bath or shower your body feels fresher and more relaxed. You have washed away all the negative energy from around your body.

On a spiritual level, Water is the element of emotion, the force of self-healing and the power of inner knowing.

Your first exercise with water is to go and sit near running water – a stream or river – or if it is not possible to find these, then a pond or lake will do.

If you are by a stream or river, look to see which way it is flowing. Is it moving fast or slowly? Is it clear or murky? What can you see in and around the water? Close your eyes and listen to the sound of the water. What kind of sound is it? How does it make you feel?

If you are by a lake or pond, then look for ripples on the surface. See if the water is clear. Can you see reflections in the water? Close your eyes and try to sense the water and any movement in it.

In both cases you could take some photos to add to your notebook.

Now it is time for an imaginary journey with the element of Water. Make sure you are sitting comfortably, relaxed and with your feet on the ground.

Imagine yourself walking by the side of a stream high up in the hills. The stream burbles as it moves rapidly over stones and around larger rocks.

You follow the path by the stream, stopping every so often to listen to the sound of the stream and the call of a few birds high in the sky. The stream goes round a bend and you follow on the twisting path.

Ahead of you, there is a wider part of the stream forming a large pool, and cascading down over a rocky ledge into the pool is a waterfall. The waterfall is about ten feet high and, as the water flows over the rocky ledge, there is a lot of spray shimmering with all the colours of the rainbow.

You pause at the bottom of the waterfall and take off your shoes. You dip your toes into the water; it is cold! So you decide to explore and as you move forwards again you see a narrow path between the rocks and the waterfall.

You step onto this narrow path, moving slowly and carefully. Looking out through the water you are amazed at the sparkles of light and rainbow colours changing rapidly as the water flows downwards. You feel refreshed and invigorated by this wonderful sight and stay there for a while.

Soon you realise that you must return to the path and return home, but you know that you will remember this experience for many years.

You return down the path and when you are home you write about your experiences in your notebook.

Water in a river is always on the move, flowing continuously towards the sea. How often do you hear the words 'Go with the flow.' What do these words mean to you?

I think it is now time to move on to the element of Fire. It may be harder to find ten facts about Fire but do try to do this.

The main fact is that Fire consumes and transforms. If you burn anything, like paper or coal, you are left with ash afterwards. So you can see how fire transforms one thing into another. Fire both creates and consumes. It is also the force of life.

On a spiritual level, fire is the element of strength, of faith and of personal power. It gives us courage and strength and enables us to recharge our energies through physical sensations. Like the phoenix which rises from the ashes of self-transformation, we too can be reborn and transform our lives through the element of Fire. Fire is the magic of the Ancients. Can you imagine how they felt when they first learned how to make fire?

We also have an inner fire, the energy that moves through our body. It keeps us steady and strong and helps us to stand up against others when needed.

So your first exercise is to stand or sit still and, with a straight back, try to sense the energy moving through your body. If you have done any martial arts you will find

19

this quite easy. Otherwise it may take some time to feel the energy moving.

Another small exercise for you now.

Light a candle or sit by a fire and concentrate on the flames for a few minutes. Notice the movement of the flame and the colours in it. Sometimes you can see images in the flames.

As I write this, Bonfire Night is less than a month away. But this year, 2012, has seen many beacons lit throughout our countryside. In ancient times, beacons were used to communicate, mainly as warnings.

Now I am going to ask you to attempt a much harder imaginary journey.

See yourself sitting in a small room with a log fire. You are sitting on the floor in front of the fire. The logs are burning brightly and you watch the flames with interest. There are many colours and shapes within the flames.

You draw nearer to the fire and, as you do so, you see an image of an old man appear in the flames. He asks you to remember all the friends and family who are no longer with you and to tell him their names. As you do this, with each name you give him, he sprinkles herbs on the logs, so they burn more brightly.

As you come to the end of the list, he speaks again, telling you that all those that have gone before you, send you

20

their love and blessings and wish you joy on this life's journey.

He then disappears and you sit for several more minutes reflecting on this experience before returning to your own room.

Don't forget to write about your experiences in your notebook.

Now it is time for us to look at how these four elements connect together.

Let's take an obvious scenario. You are camping near a river and sitting by a campfire. You have the element of Air all around you, the element of Earth under and around you, the element of Water nearby and the element of Fire in front of you. I am sure you can think of other times and places where you find all four elements together. Being a druid means being aware of all around you and how it all interconnects. What we are doing is really at quite a basic level, but you have to start somewhere.

By now you should be more aware of each of these elements and their spiritual meanings as you go about your daily life. You should also be aware of how precious each element is to us and give it the respect it deserves.

Think about your daily life and see if it has changed while you have been doing this work. Are you more aware of how you do things? Do you have more respect for the elements around you?

Write down some of these thoughts in your notebook. It may be that you have changed the way you do certain things. Note these too.

One final imaginary journey with the elements before we move on.

Imagine you are sitting outside on a summer evening by a campfire. Although it has been a warm day, the evening breeze cools the air so you sit near to the fire.

You relax and allow your eyes to close. You can hear the crackling of the flames but then you hear a light footfall and you sense that someone is standing in front of you. You open your eyes and see a figure dressed in a long cloak and holding out a bowl towards you. The bowl is earthenware and a beautiful deep brown in colour. It is filled with water.

You take the bowl and place it on the ground in front of you. Then you use your hands to splash your face with the water, tasting it as it runs down your face. The water smells and tastes fresh, as if from a spring. The figure picks up the bowl and empties it on the ground. No words are spoken but you have an inner understanding of everything that has occurred. You feel refreshed and renewed from the water.

You look up towards the fire; the figure has gone, but you know that something special has taken place.

When you return home from this imaginary journey, write about your experiences in your notebook.

Now it is time to move on and learn something else about the druids and how they work.

Lesson 3

The Directions

We are going to do some work with the directions: North, South, East and West. I can hear you saying, 'What have the directions to do with druidry?' It is an often-asked question and you will soon find out the answer.

Native Americans also work with the directions and, as in druidry, have animals associated with them.

However, an exercise first.

Draw in your notebook a large cross and mark it with N, S, E and W. Then write in the words that you associate with each direction.

On the opposite page is mine:

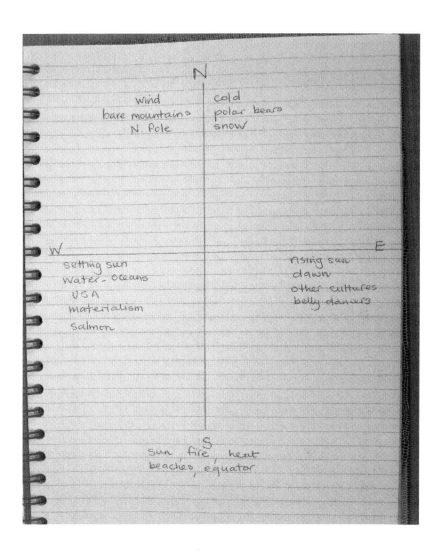

N

wind
bare mountains
N. Pole

cold
polar bears
snow

W

setting sun
water - oceans
USA
materialism

salmon

E

rising sun
dawn
other cultures
belly dancers

S

sun, fire, heat
beaches, equator

Yours may be totally different, although we may agree on some words. I only added a few but I am sure you can think of more. If you live in the southern hemisphere then your North answers would not be the same, as your S would be cold and your N warm. As I am writing this in the UK I will be discussing the directions from this viewpoint.

So let's take a look at the North first. The North is associated with the element of Earth. Animals associated with the North are the Great Bear (especially the one we see in the sky), buffalo, wolf, owl and mythic creatures like dragons.

On a spiritual level, the North teaches us wisdom and truth, responsibility and authority.

So let's take an imaginary journey to the North. Sit comfortably and relaxed, with your feet on the floor.

Imagine that it is winter time. It is very cold and there has been a heavy fall of snow. You wrap up warmly and go outside. The snow glistens in the winter sun. Everywhere looks clean and pure. The trees look beautiful too with their coating of snow.

You notice footprints in the snow and wonder who made them. They seem to have started by your front door and head towards the trees. You make sure you are still warm, then set off to follow the footprints. They go in a straight line to start with, then turn to go around the back of the trees.

You follow carefully, being aware that you may see something or someone unexpected. As you come behind the trees, the open space is filled with lights, just like the Aurora Borealis. You know this is what it is despite the fact that you generally do not see this here as you are not far enough in the North. You stop to watch the lights. They are so beautiful. You are filled with awe. But also you feel filled with strength and know that whatever happens in your life you will only have to remember this scene and you will be filled again with the strength and determination to overcome any obstacles.

After a while you start to feel cold and know that you must return home.

Once back home, you get warm by the fire and write down your feelings on this journey in your notebook.

So now let's take a look at the direction South. Look at the words you added to your chart for the South. Can you think of any others you could add?

The South is associated with the element of Fire. Animals associated with the South are bear, fox, deer and snake.

The spiritual attributes of the South are faith and trust, strength and protection. Relationships with yourself, others and with nature are also associated with the South. In the South we can learn about courage and renewal. Think about what you learned about Fire. Can you see how Fire is connected with the South?

So now let's take an imaginary journey to the South.

Imagine you are on a tropical island and heading towards the beach. Suddenly your attention is drawn to a path between some trees. There is an arrow pointing along the path. You decide to follow the path and move towards it.

The path goes through luxuriant plants and trees. The colours of the flowers are vibrant and shimmer in the heat of the sun. You can see and hear colourful birds as they move around in the trees.

You come to a fork in the path and wonder which way to go. Then you see another arrow pointing along the right-hand fork. You take this path, enjoying the vibrant life around you. Soon you come to a clearing by a small pool. There is a wooden seat waiting for you. You go towards the seat and sit down.

It is very hot and soon you close your eyes. You feel safe and protected here and the sun gives you a wonderful feeling of warmth and peace.

You hear a voice speaking to you but your eyes stay closed. Whatever words are said to you will stay in your unconscious mind but you will remember them when you are ready to hear them.

Soon you feel that it is time to return and you open your eyes. You stand and stretch. Somehow you feel different, stronger and with a better understanding of the nature around you. You also feel that you will have a better understanding of your relationships with the people around you.

You walk back along the path, through the vibrant shrubs and trees, back to where you started. You decide to return home now and write about this experience in your notebook.

The direction of East is next. Look back at the words you associated with East. Can you add more words now?

OK. Think about the East. The sun rises in the east, bringing dawn and a new day. New beginnings, then. East is associated with the element of Air so it also brings better communication. We can develop our mental and psychic work in the East.

Animals associated with the East are the hawk, eagle, deer and wolf.

If you have never watched a sunrise then this is something you should definitely do. It is very awe inspiring to watch the sun rise over the horizon, gradually spreading its light everywhere.

So now it is time to take an imaginary journey to the East. Sit comfortably, relaxed and with your feet on the floor or ground.

Imagine you are travelling through the desert for a few days to study the landscape. You are not alone but part of a small group travelling together to do the work. You have slept in your tent but have been called to go outside to watch the sun rise. The campfire is burning and the morning is chilly. You wrap a blanket around you and go to join the others around the fire. It is still dark with only the flames of the fire providing light.

You are all watching the horizon in the east. Suddenly you notice a glimmer of light. It grows slowly but steadily until the tip of the sun appears. Steadily the sun moves higher and higher until it is fully showing. Everywhere is bathed in the golden light of the sun.

You all look at each other, feeling joy and creativity. You want to paint the sunrise or write a poem about it. Instead you all get up, hold hands and dance around the fire. You are energised and focussed and want to tell the world how you feel.

Soon you realise that it is time to pack and move, to find the way home. When you all reach the edge of the desert and have to separate, you hug each other and promise to keep in touch.

When you reach your own home you get out your notebook and write or sketch the sunrise.

The last direction is West, where the sun sets. Look back at the words you wrote about the West. Can you add more?

The element associated with the West is Water. Here in the UK I always feel that this is appropriate as to the west of our island is a huge expanse of water, the Atlantic Ocean. Animals associated with the West are raven, bear and all the sea mammals.

The spiritual meanings here are emotions, dreams and healing. The West is where we can learn about all of these. We can also learn about our inner selves and how to balance our male and female energies.

So time now for our imaginary journey to the West. Sit relaxed and comfortable with your feet on the floor.

Imagine you are swimming in the sea. It is a warm sunny day with a clear blue sky. The water is warm and you enjoy swimming in the sheltered bay. You can see a small rocky island not too far away and decide to swim towards it. It does not take long and soon you are scrambling on the rocks to find somewhere to sit and and rest. You find a nice hollow where you can sit, lean back and relax in the sunshine. You close your eyes and listen to the sound of the waves against the rocks. It is a gentle splashing sound, which soothes you.

Then unexpectedly you hear voices singing, an ethereal melody which soars high then dips low. It is the most amazing sound you have ever heard. Occasionally you hear a word or two. The words seem to have no real meaning but you start to feel a deep sense of peace, and things that had been worrying you fade into insignificance. You feel as if something has shifted inside you and there is a sense of balance.

When the singing stops, you know it is time to go. You open your eyes but can see no-one around. You clamber down the rocks into the sea and swim back to the beach. You keep thinking about this experience on your way home and hurry to write about it in your notebook before you forget it.

We have now looked at the four directions, North, South, East and West.

For now you need a double-page spread in your notebook. Divide it into five sections horizontally, with the narrowest section at the top, and six columns vertically.

Here is mine:

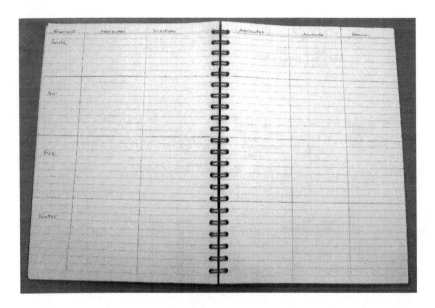

I have put in the headings for the columns and for the horizontal sections as you can see. The second column, headed 'attributes', is for the words associated with each element, lining them up in the correct sections. Then you can add the directions for each element and the attributes of the directions. The next column is for the animals associated with each of these. The final column is headed 'seasons', which we will be coming to next. Leave two more pages free as this chart will expand quite rapidly soon.

Now for a final little exercise:

In the morning, stand outside if possible. Face the East and acknowledge the fact that the sunrise brings a new day. Be thankful for this because of the opportunities it brings. Now turn to the South and acknowledge the sun which brings warmth. Then turn to the West and acknowledge the power of water and a thankfulness for water, as it without we cannot live. Finally, turn to the North and acknowledge the strength and determination brought by the North.

If you do this each morning, your day will be calmer and any problems will be easier to deal with. Try it and see, and write about it in your notebook too. Something else you can do is find out about the animals associated with each direction, especially their strengths.

Lesson 4

The Seasons

We all know what the seasons are and in druidry the seasons are very important. We go from Winter to Spring, from Spring to Summer, from Summer to Autumn, and then from Autumn to Winter again. The seasons form a cycle and this is known as the Wheel of the Year.

First of all let's compare Summer and Winter.

Make two columns in your notebook, one headed Summer, the other Winter. Use words and phrases to describe these seasons, placing them in the correct column. For example, in the Summer column you could write: hot, sunny, flowers in bloom; and under the Winter heading you could write: cold, icy, snow, bare trees.

Have a really good think about this and take some time to do the exercise. A hint – where is the sun placed in the sky in summer and in winter?

Now make two more columns and do the same for Spring and Autumn.

By now you should have a really good idea of how things change from season to season. There is a distinct cycle of growth which can be observed, like the new buds in Spring, becoming leaves in Summer and changing colour and dying in the Autumn. Can you see any other growth cycles during the year? Make a note of any that you think about.

Let's look at Winter first. Using the words and phrases from your Winter column, write a paragraph describing Winter.

Here is mine:

'During Winter, the days are short and the nights long. The sun is low in the sky and dazzles you when walking outside. It is cold but the air feels crisper and cleaner. The plants have died down and the trees are bare, their outlines stark against the sky. Many animals have hibernated and at times I feel that way myself. The land seems dormant but it is not as it seems. The long evenings bring opportunities to think and plan for the Spring.'

I could write more but thought that was enough for one paragraph.

Druids celebrate the seasons, generally with a ceremony or gathering. The Winter festival is called Samhain, pronounced 'Sow(as in cow)–in' and is from 31st October to 2nd November. In ancient times, all the crops would have been gathered in and stored. Any animals not needed were slaughtered and salted to provide meat during the winter. It was a time of change from one way of living to another.

Samhain coincides with Hallowe'en, and the Christian All Saints or All Hallows Day. It is a time when it is easier to connect with the ancient ones, our ancestors, as the veil between their world and ours is thinner at this time. It is a time when we honour the ancestors and the loved ones we have lost. The ancients believed that their ancestors would visit at this time and would set a place for them at the table.

Hallowe'en games are based on old rituals. The apple is a sacred fruit and also magical, meaning immortality, death and rebirth. If you cut an apple across the core, you will see a hidden five-pointed star revealed, a sign of deep mysteries.

This is the time to connect to the Earth, to feel the energy of the Earth and also a time to look deep inside yourself. This is the time also for working on yourself, looking at how you live your life and looking for ways to make your life better and more fulfilling.

The long nights of sleep renew our physical bodies and so it becomes easier to see new ways of living, finding things to get rid of, things we no longer need, so there is a place for the new. Many of us fear change and get stuck in a rut. This is the time to see a way through, trusting our intuition to find new insight on our path through life. There are lots of things to do during this time.

- *Write on a piece of paper the things you want to get rid of, then burn them safely.*
- *Place photos or other items that remind you of your ancestors on a small table and light a candle for them.*
- *Visit ancient burial mounds.*
- *Help the birds to survive the winter by placing food and water out for them.*
- *Do a review of the previous 12 months, note any changes in your life, sort out old clothes and household items for charity shops or recycling.*
- *Learn to meditate.*

Some trees are special to Samhain. One is the elder, which is considered to be a tree of wisdom and regeneration. The other tree is the yew, which is a powerful symbol of death and rebirth and of total transformation.

Find out more about these trees and see if you can find them so you can take photographs of them for your notebook.

So time now for another imaginary journey in the winter time. Sit in a comfortable position with your feet on the ground.

Imagine yourself working outside on a cold winter's day. There are sheep to check and chickens to make safe in their coop. It is already getting dark and you hurry to make sure all the animals are safe before returning to your cosy warm cottage.

You add more logs to the fire and as you get warm you begin to feel drowsy and close your eyes.

It has been a hard day and you start to think about all the things you need to do before the spring. It is a long list. You hear a voice and sense a presence in the room. 'Only do that which is essential,' you hear. The voice sounds like that of an old man, perhaps an ancient ancestor. 'Use your time wisely,' the voice continues. 'Let go of that which you do not need.' There is a pause before the voice continues, 'Choose your friends wisely too; also let those go who no longer have your trust. Stay true to yourself, plan carefully for the coming Spring and you will find fulfilment.'

The voice stops and you feel the presence go away. 'Thank you,' you whisper. When you awake, you remember the voice and the words and spend some time thinking about them and how you could make the changes to your life so that your life is easier and more fulfilling.

In your notebook, jot down some of your own thoughts on this.

The next season is, of course, Spring. To me there is something special about the Spring. I love to see new life beginning and the longer days. Look at your Spring words and write a paragraph about the Spring.

The festival of Spring is on the 1st and/or 2nd February. The Christians call it Candlemas when it is celebrated by candlelight. It is also St. Brigid's Day, but the Druids call it Imbolc (pronounced Im-olc).

As I said earlier, it is the time when the days get longer and the sun slowly moves higher in the sky. It is as if everything is quickening; you can feel the first stirrings of Spring, see the snowdrops peeping out, hear the birds singing more and see the buds appearing on some trees.

Imbolc celebrates the return of the goddess to the land. Brighid, Brigit or Bride is associated with the Sacred Fire, the fertile earth, healing, poetry and the art of smithing.

It is a time for us to prepare for the changes to come, to spring clean, not only our homes but also our minds. Clearing out the old makes space for the new and this includes ideas and methods that no longer work for us.

We can create things, meditate, write poetry, bringing our creativity out of the dark, like the plants pushing their heads through the soil. All the ideas and plans you made during the Winter can now be brought out, ready to work on so as that they grow and prosper.

The willow tree is associated with Spring. It always seems to look green before any of the other trees. Willow brings intuition and allows your projects to move forward.

Another tree associated with the Spring is the rowan. Rowan can help you to find answers by looking within. It also helps you to heal old wounds, a kind of spiritual cleansing.

One of the early Spring plants is coltsfoot. This is a herb which can be used as a remedy to help clear the lungs. The leaves can also be used as an incense.

There are lots of Spring activities:

- *Have a long bath surrounded by candlelight.*
- *Drink fresh spring water all day.*
- *Use a small table for items that represent the Spring.*
- *Spring clean.*
- *Plant new bushes and shrubs.*
- *Clear out unwanted items, clothes, books, bric-a-brac and recycle or donate to charity shops.*

Try to do at least three of these activities and write about your feelings afterwards.

So now an imaginary journey during the Spring time. Make

sure you are sitting in a relaxed and comfortable position with your feet on the ground.

Imagine you are walking along a narrow lane. It is quite cold but the sun is shining and you feel a hint of warmth from the sun. The trees are still bare but here and there you can see buds appearing. You look to see if you can identify them and feel pleased when you can. Under the bare hedges you see a tiny flower appearing, then another. They are snowdrops. You feel heartened by this as you know that summer will soon be here.

The lane turns a corner and starts to rise. It is not a steep climb but a gradual one. Soon you leave the trees and hedges behind and come onto open land.

There are gentle hills and you can see pockets of snow lying in some of the hollows. You carry on up the lane and you start to feel a breeze which had been hidden by the trees and hedges.

Eventually you reach the top of the lane. There is a gate. You open it and go through carefully closing the gate afterwards.

You are nearly on top of the hill so you head towards it. You feel a spring in your step as the grass under you gives you a helping 'hand' to move forwards.

At the top of the hill is a cairn. You sit in the shelter of the cairn and look around you at the view. You can see sheep in the distance and smoke rising from a cottage chimney.

You feel energised from your walk. Your mind is clear, the breeze having blown away any negative energy around you. You sit and make plans for when you return home. You can see there is a lot to do, cleaning out unwanted items so you will have room for new projects and activities.

After a while, the sun disappears and you know you must return home. You stand and stretch, then retrace your steps down the hill, through the gate and down the lane.

When you get home you hurry to write your thoughts and ideas in your notebook.

Next is the season of Summer.

Look at your Summer words and write a paragraph about Summer.

Here in the UK we often have wet and cool summers.. The year 2012 was extremely wet with floods in many places. But in our minds, we see Summer as hot and sunny, with all the flowers and trees in full bloom. It is a time when we can sit outside or visit the beach and relax.

For Druids, the season of Summer begins on 1st May. It is known as Beltane. Beltane can be spelt in many ways, Beltaine, Bealteinne, or Belteine. The word itself means 'May Day' in Scottish Gaelic but its original meaning is 'The Good Fire' or the 'Bel-fire'. Bel, a Celtic god, was the 'Bright One' - the god of light and fire. Bel-fires were lit on hilltops to celebrate the coming of life and fertility with the warmth of the sun.

The major feature of the Beltane festival was the jumping over the fire. People jumped over the fire to bring themselves a partner, or for a safe journey while travelling or to ensure fertility and for many other reasons.

So Beltane is a time when fertility is the main theme. May Day is when we dance around the Maypole, itself a symbol of fertility, and also a time of other ritual dances and games. Beltane marks the beginning of Summer and it is the time when the cattle were taken to the summer pastures until Samhain. But first the cattle were driven through Beltane fires to ensure their fertility.

This festival also celebrates love, courtship and the rising tide of the life force. Many villages chose a May King and a May Queen and these were both crowned on May Day. Some villages still do this.

Things that you can do:

- *Walk barefoot in the grass.*
- *Watch the Moon rise as the Sun sets.*
- *Dance or do a walking meditation.*
- *Do something creative which you don't usually do.*
- *Spend time in the garden watching the bees do their work.*
- *Spend some time looking at the points of view of the opposite sex.*
- *Join new groups.*
- *Enter a competition.*
- *Visit sacred wells and springs.*
- *Make a pilgrimage or sacred journey.*

- *Make a shrine using Spring flowers and other suitable Beltane items.*
- *Wear green in honour of the Earth.*

The tree associated with Beltane is the Hawthorn. This is the May tree and its blossom can be given as a token of friendship or love. The blossom can be used as a tea for a Spring tonic which will help the heart and circulation. Hawthorn also indicates a time of cleansing and a time when new positive energies will enter your life, rewarding you for past actions. Meditating with Hawthorn will help you to realise a new potential.

The herbs associated with this time are rosemary and the cowslip. (Not many people realise that the cowslip can be used as a herb.)

Cowslips were often given as a token of friendship. It is a safe herb to use with babies, children and the elderly. It can be used for mild insomnia and headaches. It will also calm a dry irritating cough.

Rosemary is a symbol of fertility and is used in handfasting ceremonies. It can also be burnt as an incense. It can be made into a tea which can also be used as an antiseptic on wounds or to ease muscular pains. **Do not use if you have high blood pressure or if you are pregnant.**

Now here is a short meditation for Beltane.

Sit comfortably and take several deep breaths to quieten your mind. See yourself walking across the village green, moving away from the crowds and heading towards a small wood.

As you approach the wood you notice that it seems full of light and you stop for a few moments, looking into the wood in wonder. Inside you can see a figure of light which gradually changes into a lady, clothed in a green velvet cloak. She beckons you forward and you move towards her, stopping just in front of her. She does not speak, but you sense her sending love and healing towards you. Anything that has been troubling you disappears and you feel a sense of inner peace. She offers you a branch of May blossom. You take it and immediately feel its effects, both cleansing and energising. The lady disappears and you sit down, still holding the blossom. You think about the meaning of the blossom and of this time of the year. You think of what you need to do to make your life richer and more fulfilled.

The wood seems darker now and you know it is time to return. You get up and stretch, then leave the wood and return to the village, carrying your May blossom safely home.

Now it is time to write about this experience.

We started with the Winter season and now we come to Autumn, the time of the harvest. For me, in the UK, I feel that our real harvest does not start until later than the date for the festival of Lughnasadh.

Look back at your words about Autumn and write a paragraph about this season.

Lughnasadh (loo-na-sa) is often spelled in other ways, such as Lughnasa and Lughnasagh, and is also known as Lammas. It marks the time of the beginning of the harvest and is a time of joy; but it is also a time when we prepare for Autumn and the approaching Winter. Lughnasadh itself means 'the commemoration of Lugh'. Lugh is a god of fire and light and in Irish legend was the leader of the tribe Tuatha De Danann. In the story of their victory over the Fomors, Lugh spares the life of Bres, the captured enemy leader, in exchange for advice on ploughing, sowing and reaping.

Lugh was the patron deity of many towns and was the spiritual father of CuChulain. He is also analogous to Llew in Welsh myth.

The theme of sacrifice is important at this time and Lugh undergoes death and rebirth in a sacrificial mating with the Goddess. The corn is cut down and is reborn as the loaf of bread. This is the time when the god dies but also releases his seed, to be reborn again. This is the time which is depicted in the story of Taliesin, when Gwion dies as a seed and is swallowed by Ceridwen which leads to his rebirth as Taliesin. Lugh is John Barleycorn whose energy has gone into the grain, is cut down and sacrificed back to the land.

Lughnasadh is a turning point in the year, the point when you reap the fruits of your actions. The harvest is both a time of death and achievement. Sacrifice can be seen as letting go of something in order to move to a higher or deeper level. This festival can be seen as a time of transformation, as the corn is transformed into bread.

Lughnasadh is also the celebration of the Corn or Grain Mother. On Lughnasadh Eve, fires were lit on mounds such as Silbury Hill to honour the Corn Mother as she gives birth to her harvest child, the Grain. This is the seed which brings forth the next year's harvest.

There are many old customs regarding the first and last sheaf of corn to be cut. The last sheaf was often cut by the youngest girl present and fashioned into a corn maiden. It was taken joyfully back to the village and hung over the fireplace. It was later burnt on the Lammas fire. Sometimes the corn maidens or dollies were kept until Yule when they were divided up amongst the cattle, or at times they were kept until the Spring. In Scotland the young maid was made from the last stalks cut, and the old wife from the first stalks cut. The old wife was passed to the nearest farmer who had not yet harvested his corn and so on until it reached the last farm to cut the corn.

Lughnasadh was a time for feasting, dancing and merry-making, a celebration of the first harvest and it could last a whole month.

Lughnasadh also represents a change in the energy; it is from now that we see the first signs of change and death. The first fruits are being gathered and we start to think of laying in stores for the winter. We can gather in our own harvest, the harvest of our desires and the fruits of our labours. We can begin to understand on the inner levels what we have done on the outer levels. It is a time when we can start the reflective process, as well as giving thanks for all the rewards we are harvesting.

Things you can do:

- *Bake a Lammas loaf.*
- *Cut your hair.*
- *Dance or do a movement meditation.*
- *Observe an ear of corn or a sheaf of wheat. See the finer details and meditate on it.*
- *Have a Lughnasadh fire.*
- *Weave a corn dolly.*
- *Create a shrine to the Corn Mother Goddess and the Corn God.*
- *Make a staff of hazel.*
- *Read the story of Taliesin.*

The tree most associated with this time is the Hazel. Hazel is native to the British Isles. It flowers in February and March and later bears edible nuts which provide food for small animals. In Celtic legend, nine nuts of wisdom fell from the Hazel tree into the river. They were eaten by a magical salmon who absorbed all the wisdom and changed into a young girl. Hazel brings help towards an intuitive path. Hazel also helps you to attune to the cyclic changes within nature and will draw your attention to the things which need your care.

Gorse, though not a tree, is also associated with this time. In Celtic legend, Gorse is linked to wisdom which comes as a result of hard work. Gorse helps to restore faith and hope if you feel down and will help you to find new approaches to your life. Gorse is found on moorland and common land and flowers for much of the year. Carry a sprig of gorse with you to help you focus on your own harvest.

There are two herbs for this festival or season: sage and meadowsweet.

Sage is associated with wisdom and releasing blocks in expression. It is connected to the throat chakra so it helps you to express your emotions. Sage is best harvested before it flowers and can be used to make herb tea. It can also be used as an antiseptic herb or as a gargle. It can be burned as an incense to purify and cleanse but **it must not be taken if pregnant or for long periods of time**.

Garlands of meadowsweet were traditionally worn for Lughnasadh celebrations. Its perfume expands the psyche and builds a connection to the source. It enhances flexibility and connection to the inner levels. It can be used as a sedative and painkiller (as it is natural aspirin) and is a good digestive tonic. It is good for any inflammatory condition, is a strong diuretic and helps immune system function. It is best harvested just as the flowers are beginning to open. **Don't use this if on anti-coagulant drugs.**

So now to a brief meditation for this season.

Sit comfortably and take a few deep breaths.

See yourself sitting in a corner of a field which has been harvested. The ground now is almost bare with stubble showing in the soil. It is quiet and peaceful and you close your eyes. You sense people arriving. They lay a gift at your feet, then move away to form a circle around you. This procession of people goes on for some time but you do not open your eyes.

When you sense that no-one else will come you open your eyes and look around you. In front of you is a display of gifts from Nature's harvest. There are many and you try to commit these gifts to memory. There are also other gifts which you cannot see, but you can sense them. The people in the circle are all smiling. You smile back and thank them for their wonderful gifts. They fade away and you are left alone with the gifts. These also fade away and you are left to contemplate their meaning. You start to think about these gifts and what kind of gifts you can give to others. The gifts you have received remain in your memory and in your heart. Use them wisely.

You start to feel chilly and know it is time to return. You walk back home and write about the wonderful gifts you received and those you can give to others.

We have now covered the four seasons of the year and four of the festivals. There are four other festivals to celebrate and these come in the next lesson. You will then see how they all fit into the wheel of the year. But before we continue, look back at your notes and reflect how you can work with the seasons in your own life. You can find out more about the legends associated with these four festivals. You can also add more to your chart that you started in Lesson 3.

Lesson 5

The Wheel of the Year and the other four festivals

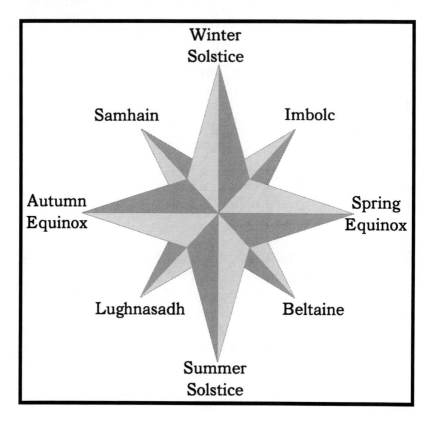

There are two solstice festivals, one for the shortest day and one for the longest day, and two equinox festivals where day and night are equal in length. Our first festival is the Winter Solstice, or Alban Arthuan or Yule

Alban Arthuan means the 'Light of Arthur'. Arthur here, is

aligned with the Sun God who dies and is reborn at the Winter Solstice. In Celtic myth, it is said that he is sleeping in a secret cave in the Welsh mountains and will one day awake and return to save our isles.

This is an essential theme of this festival – the apparent death of the sun and its rebirth when the need-fire is lit, which celebrates the return of Arthur by association. The theme of the dying Sun God being reborn at this time is found in many cultures and religions.

The Sun God Mithras was born at this time, the time of the shortest day and the longest night. Ancient sites, such as Stonehenge and New Grange, are often oriented towards the sunset and the sunrise of the Winter Solstice sun.

During a Solstice ceremony, all the lights are put out at a certain point, and then the Solstice light is lit and all other lights lit from the Solstice light. Essential features of this are the mourning for that which is finishing and dying, a period of inner darkness and a recognition of the reality of rebirth. Rebirth can only happen when we have fully mourned or recognised the passing of the old (letting go of the old to make space for the new).

The Solstice is a moment to stop, to look backwards in reflection and look forward to a new active season as the Sun brings increasing warmth and daylight. The previous time, from Samhain to this Solstice, is a period of darkness, of inner work, dreaming, preparing for the rebirth of action at the Winter Solstice. Inner journeys bring wisdom and understanding, and at the Solstice we celebrate the rebirth of the balance of power to humanity as a whole.

As the Sun's rebirth is celebrated, life becomes active again. It is time to bring forward our visions into the light, for naming our dreams and helping them to manifest. It is the time of the year when I personally rejoice as I know the days will now get longer. This brings hope and renewal into my life.

Things you can do:

- *Bring evergreens into the home; they represent everlasting life.*
- *Make wreaths or wheels.*
- *Make a Yule log, traditionally oak. Use it to clear thoughts and energies you wish to purify, transform and release.*
- *Buy or make special candles.*
- *Cleanse your aura, rooms and crystals with sage smoke.*

As with the four main festivals there are trees associated with these festivals too. The trees for this time of the year are the birch and fir/pine trees. I love the birch tree, so gentle and ladylike yet strong and able to withstand harsh conditions. The birch tree was one of the first trees to recolonise after the Ice Age.

Birch indicates new beginnings. But you need to get rid of any negative energies first. Birch helps with perception so that you can gain new understanding and peace of mind.

Fir and pine trees indicate rebirth and transformation. Fir enables you to stay rooted in the Earth but allows you to see into the distance where new knowledge will be gained.

Having got this far in the lesson, how has your life changed? Do you do things in a different way? Do you see things differently? Do you feel different?

Write some notes on your answers to these questions. After the next short mediation you may like to go back to these notes and see if your answers have changed.

Sit comfortably and take a few deep breaths.

See yourself sitting on a tree stump in the woods. It is dark, not yet dawn. You wrap your cloak or blanket firmly around you to keep out the cold. As your eyes grow accustomed to the darkness you begin to see movement in the trees. There is a dark figure hiding behind a large tree. There is silence and there is no more movement.

You become aware of a glimmer of light which appears then disappears through the trees. But it grows stronger each time it appears. This continues until the light reaches the dark figure. Now it is dawn and time for the light to return. The dark figure is enveloped in the light and shines out, bringing the light to the whole wood.

You feel renewed and energised by the light and you sense that all the plans you have made for the Spring time will come to fruition. You think about these now, and then, with a spring in your step, you get up and leave the woods, going home to write about this experience.

Our second festival is the Spring Equinox, which comes between Imbolc and Beltane.

This festival is known as Alban Eilir and occurs around 21/22 March. Alban Eilir translates as 'Light of the Earth'. It is the time of equal day and night but a time of looking forward to longer days. Everything in nature is awakening at this time. The sun is gaining strength and the days grow longer and warmer. Catkins and blossom can be seen on the trees as well as buds, while spring flowers show themselves and lambs appear in the fields.

It is time to reach out for what we want for ourselves and the world; time to begin new ventures, journey and make plans. It is time also to work towards balance in ourselves which will bring healing and change into our lives. We can look forward with joy to the months still to come and celebrate this time. The symbolic plant for Alban Eilir is the trefoil or shamrock. This plant is worn on St. Patrick's day, which is on 17th March, very near to the Equinox. The three leaves of the shamrock symbolise the Trinity but also the Triple Goddess; Artemis, Triple Moon Goddess of the Greeks. She fed her hinds on trefoil.

Oestre, the Goddess of Light, is also associated with this festival as she brings fertility in the Spring.

There are many symbols of balance. How many of the following have you seen or know about? Find a picture of each or draw them, then study them carefully. What does the symbol mean to you?

Make notes on your thoughts.

- Celtic Cross
- Caduceus
- Entwined serpent
- Spiral
- Triskelion or Triple spiral
- 6-pointed star
- Yin and Yang

There are many other things you can do at this time too.

- *Plant seeds.*
- *Decorate hens' eggs.*
- *Make flags to fly in the wind and to carry your prayers around the world.*
- *Create a shrine which reflects balance, awakening and new life.*
- *Meditate with trees.*
- *Continue to let go of things which you no longer need.*
- *Make plans for the coming months: journeys, new projects, etc.*

The trees for Alban Eilir are the ash and the alder.

Ash is native to the British Isles and flourishes best on limestone soil in wetter regions. Its wood has been used to make oars, spears and handles for tools, as well as furniture and carts.

Ash asks you to look at the wider picture of whatever is troubling you. Stand back and look at your actions and thoughts so that you get a clear view of where you want to go. Ash helps you also to balance your inner and outer selves.

Alder is common in Britain, growing on wet soils by rivers and retaining brown cone-like fruits in the Winter. Ancient man saw the alder as sacred because it appeared to bleed when cut, as its sap turned red when exposed to the air.

Alder offers protection in conflicts and helps you to free yourself from things that bind you. Alder gives you moral and physical strength and is linked with emotions.

Herbs for this festival are nettle and hyssop. Nettle is a Spring tonic. Nettle tea cleanses the blood and tones up the whole system. Nettle is rich in iron.

Hyssop is a herb of purification, used to cleanse temples and sacred places, long ago. It balances the emotions, warms and strengthens. It can be used as a tea or as an incense.

Now it is time for a brief meditation on the Spring Equinox, Alban Eilir.

Sit comfortably and take a few deep breaths.

You see yourself walking along a path by a small stream. The stream makes burbling noises as it flows over small rocks. It is sunny and there are reflections in the stream. You feel peaceful.

The path moves away from the stream and leads you towards a small clump of bushes and small trees. You can see buds and small catkins on the trees. These are the signs of Spring. Nature renews itself each year and so do you. Feel the energy from the earth and trees bringing a renewed feeling of vitality into your body. What will you do with this vitality, this renewal of energy? Where will it take you? You sit down on the ground. There is much to think about now. How can you work with this renewal in your life?

Think too about the stream. It flows on, around obstacles, taking with it the debris in its water, leaving clear water behind. How does this idea fit in with your life?

You sit for a while in contemplation. When you feel it is time to leave, you stand up and stretch, then return along the path to your home where you write quickly about everything that has been brought to your attention.

So now let's move on to the next festival, the Summer Solstice, Alban Heruin on 21/22 June.

The Summer Solstice on 21/22 June in the northern hemisphere is known as Alban Heruin – 'The Light of Summer'. At this time of the longest day, or maximum light, we celebrate the strength and power of the sun and the richness of the |Earth. After this time, the days grow shorter once again.

In ancient times, Alban Heruin was celebrated with bonfires on hilltops and much dancing and singing. Many people went and still go to Stonehenge or other stone circles which are aligned to the sunrise, to watch the sun rise above the stones. Vigils are still kept by modern-day druids at such places as Glastonbury Tor to await the rising of the sun.

Alban Heruin is a dual celebration. Not only does it celebrate the day of maximum light and all that has become manifest during the lengthening days, but it also celebrates the start of the return to the shorter days, the time of inner development.

It is a time to celebrate what you have achieved and manifested, a time of fulfilment, a time to celebrate who and what you are.

Things you can do:

- *Hold your own vigil.*
- *Get out in the sun.*
- *Meditate.*
- *Read inspiring texts.*
- *Dance in the sun.*
- *Visit a stone circle and spend some time there in meditation'*
- *Make a shrine to the sun.*
- *Make herb pillows or herb sachets.*

The tree for this festival is the oak. The oak is considered to be the king of the trees. It grows in lowland forests and can live to an age of 800 or more years. The oak is a tree of strength and endurance. Meditating with oak can help you to overcome whatever is troubling you or overcome any obstacles in your path. The power of oak acts as a doorway into other worlds. If you feel you would benefit from such a journey, ask oak to provide you with the doorway to a world which will give you strength and courage.

The herbs for Alban Heruin are elderflower and lavender.

Use elderflowers to make a tonic tea or a skin tonic. Infusions are good for promoting peaceful sleep, for cough and sinus problems.

Make lavender tea to relieve stress and exhaustion. Use in the bath or burn as incense, promoting clarity of thought and focussing the mind.

Now your meditation for this time, but before we start let us take a look at the two solstices again. How do you feel about these two solstice festivals? What do they mean to you? Is there any special significance for you at either of these times?

Now sit comfortably and take a few deep breaths.

You see yourself sitting on top of a hill. It is night-time but dawn is not far away. You feel a sense of anticipation as you sense the sun rising above the horizon.

It appears slowly, bringing both light and warmth. As the sun grows large, it also grows stronger.

Now the dawn chorus of the birds has begun. It is a joyous sound. You achieved this year. Everything that you have done flashes like a film in front of your eyes. What wonderful things you have achieved.

You feel a bit overwhelmed by all of this and continue to sit down in the warmth and light of the sun. When you wake you know it is time to return and go down the hill to your home where you can think about your achievements and write them down in your notebook.

Our last festival to place in our wheel of the year is the Autumn Equinox, Alban Elued, which occurs around 21st September.

The harvest is now being completed and the hours of day and night are equal. But whereas at the Spring Equinox we were looking forward to the days getting longer, now we are looking for the days to get shorter. It is a time when we reflect on all that we have gained or learned during the previous year. It is a time of contemplation and thanksgiving too, and as the days are getting shorter and darker, we need to react to this change. The harvest is now all in and has been celebrated all over our country. The schools often have harvest festivals too. It is a beautiful time of the year with so many colours in the natural life around us.

Things you can do:

- *Collect leaves and cones.*
- *Press leaves for later use.*
- *Make jams and jellies from hedgerow fruits.*
- *Make wine from hedgerow fruits.*
- *Set up a small table with items representing Autumn.*
- *Take cuttings of plants and put in pots to root.*
- *Check your store cupboard and replenish if necessary.*
- *Enjoy walks in the woods.*

As the ground rests and the animals go into hibernation, so we can bring ourselves into balance and honour our whole selves together with all of life. We too can hibernate by looking inward and reconnecting with our inner selves and our inner wisdom. The tree associated with this festival is the apple. We all know the saying 'an apple a day keeps the doctor away', I am sure. Crab apples can also be used to make wine and jelly but they are too bitter to eat on their own. Wine, of course, can be made with most types of apple. Apple offers healing and regeneration, both in body and mind. Try meditating with apple and see how much help you can receive, so that your inner and outer selves become harmonised. If you cut an apple in half, across not down, you can see the pentacle outlined in the seed area of the apple core.

Heather is also connected with this festival. Heather is abundant throughout Western Europe growing profusely in acid soil. It produces distinctive bell-like flowers in pink and mauve. Some heathers produce white flowers which are considered to be lucky. So heather can bring luck into your life. It can also help in healing.

Now it is time for a brief meditation on the Autumn Equinox.

Sit comfortably and take a few deep breaths.

You see yourself walking slowly through the woodland. The leaves are turning from green to red, brown and gold. Some have already fallen to the ground, forming a carpet. It is cooler now and you can sense a small hint of the approaching winter, but the sun is still shining.

The trees are letting go of their leaves, clearing their branches so there will be room for new growth in the spring. They are getting in balance. Are you in balance? If not, why not? And how can you find balance in your life?

Take some time now to think about this. How are you

going to reconnect with your inner self? Do you listen to your inner self?

As you walk along the path circling gently through the trees, you find the answers appearing to you. Note them now so that when you return you can write them down. As you leave the wood, thank the trees for their wisdom.

And so the Wheel of the Year turns again and we are back to Samhain. As I look back over the last few years, I can see how my knowledge has deepened as each festival comes along. I see new things each time and find deeper meanings in the old knowledge. This is the meaning of working with the Wheel of the Year, to me at least. It is more of a spiral and each time you go round you learn something new. It is a never-ending learning curve, spiral or circle, however you see it.

Now is the time for you to look back at all you have learned so far. How have you integrated this new knowledge into your everyday life? Make notes on the answer to this question so that you are ready to move on to the next lesson. You can also add more to your chart that you started in Lesson 3.

Lesson 6

Sacred Space

This lesson moves on to something new but which is very important in druidry, and that is the Spirit of Place and Sacred Space.

The whole Earth is sacred, but there are some places or points on the Earth which are felt to be especially connected to certain aspects of divine power. These places sometimes have stone circles or groves of trees or even monuments on them.

Where we are born and where we live now all influence who we are, how we think, feel and behave. We know when we have found the right place to live or work. It is also important that we put furniture, plants and trees in the right place too. How often do we move furniture around because it doesn't feel right or change the way our garden feels and looks?

Each place has a spirit, even the corner of your garden. You can work with the Spirit of Place to help cleanse and purify the environment.

Visiting sacred sites is a way of honouring the Spirit of Place. Pilgrimages to Mecca, the Ganges, Lourdes and Glastonbury all honour and respect the spirit of these places.

In a circle, the Spirit of Place is represented by a line which links East and West and is governed by the rising and setting sun, as are our days. East represents lands far distant and from which enlightenment comes. West represents the 'Isles of the

Blessed', the place where we go after death; the Summerland; a place of rest and contentment.

So how do we work with the Spirit of Place?

Sit comfortably and close your eyes.

Become aware of the Spirit of Place in this room.
What does it feel like?
What is its quality?

Move your awareness outside into the garden.
What does it feel like now?

Move your awareness to all of the town.
What does it feel like?
What is its quality?

Move your awareness to all of the British Isles.
What does it feel like?
What is its quality?

Expand your awareness now to the whole world and ask the same questions.

If you feel ready, move your awareness to the whole universe and again ask the same questions.

When you feel ready, bring your awareness back to you and write down your experiences so that you do not forget them.

Things that you can do:

- Visit nearby ancient sites. Sit there for a while and feel the energy that comes from them. Make an effort to communicate with the Spirit of Place at each site. Write down your experiences and compare with other visits to the same place.
- Find any special places in your home or garden where you can feel the Spirit of Place. Meditate in these places and again write down your experiences.

Now you can learn to work with the trees around you, maybe in your local park.

Trees, as you have probably already noticed, are important to druids.

Before any kind of communication with a tree, always ask permission of the Tree Spirit to enter its space. If permission is refused, find another tree or return at a later date. Once permission is given there are many ways to communicate with your tree. You will sense the answer so do not worry about it.

When you hug a tree, you can feel its energy, energy drawn up from the Earth and down from the Sun and Sky. This energy is a healing energy and it enables you to feel more balanced and gain a greater understanding of the world. Earth energy is also grounding, so if you have been feeling 'spaced-out' it will help you to regain your balance. However, if you are normally very down-to-earth and practical then the energy of the tree, which is coming down through the leaves and trunk, can give your spirit a lift and bring out your creative and intuitive abilities.

65

Hugging a tree does not just provide you with energy though. It is an opportunity to talk to the Tree Spirit. Put your face against the bark and tell the Tree Spirit how you feel; treat the Tree Spirit as you would a good friend. Then listen to what the Tree Spirit may tell you. This may not be in words but as feelings or as a picture in your mind. You may see, hear or feel nothing, but later ideas and thoughts may come to you in dreams or when you are sitting quietly. These ideas and thoughts will have been given to you by the Tree Spirit when you made contact. When you have finished listening to the Tree Spirit, remember to thank it for its help.

Gifting is a Native American tradition; they gift trees with cornmeal because this is sacred to them. You could use cornmeal or some other suitable gift, such as feathers, a crystal or a special stone. You could also sing a song, read a poem or play some music for your chosen tree. While you do this, you can thank the Tree Spirit for any help you have been given. Respect and love for the Tree Spirit are very important.

Asking and gifting can be combined. Ask with love and respect for what you need, explaining why you need this at this time. Listen to what the Tree Spirit may have to tell you. Always remember to thank the Tree Spirit even if you hear nothing at that time.

Many of you will already have a special bag in which you keep items which hold a special meaning for you. If you do not have one, then they are easy to make. You can make one with a flap or one from a circular piece of material and a drawstring to keep it closed. Whatever you do, do not rush this, as when you make it you put in energy to the creation of your bag. In your bag you can keep special tree items, such as cones, dried leaves, dried fruits or small pieces of bark. For extra help, either wear your bag for a few days or tie it to your favourite tree or Prayer Tree. If you do this a few days before the Full Moon and remove it the day after the Full Moon then its powers will be enhanced.

When offering prayers and invocations outside with your tree, always begin by centering yourself then hugging your tree if permission has been granted for you to do so. When you have finished, remember to thank the Tree Spirit and leave a small gift.

Here are a few suggestions for you.

First of all, look back through your notes to find which trees are good for your purpose; for example, working with the birch tree can help you to start new projects. Oak is a tree which will give you protection. Carrying a small oak twig with you offers protection at all times.

All trees will offer you wisdom but Fir is best. You can burn fir needles (safely in a container) and waft the smoke over you.

Willow is the best tree to ask for help with intuition and psychic abilities. Here is a little prayer or invocation which you can say if you walk around the willow tree. Touch the branches gently as well.

O Spirit of Willow
Allow your energies
To flow towards me
Through me, touching
And inspiring.

Smudging is a way of purifying and cleansing. Birch, Hawthorn and Elder will all aid cleansing. Dried leaves, twigs and bark can be burned for purification. Waft the smoke over and around you, at the same time asking the Tree Spirits to cleanse you of any negative thoughts and feelings. When you have finished, remember to thank the Tree Spirits.

Work through as many of the above suggestions as you need to and write down how you feel and what you experienced. These are things you can do over and over again. As you read more and experience more, you can add to the chart which you started in Lesson 3.

We have now come to the end of these lessons for beginners. I hope that you have gained knowledge and guidance through the work you have done during this time. The content of these lessons is only a beginning and if you want to learn more there are many books you can read and courses you can do. An internet search will bring up many treasures, far more than I could recommend here. I wish you many blessings on this continuing journey.

I would love to hear how you have got on with these lessons. I can be contacted on gladysdinnacombe@btinternet.com

Other resources

Websites:

The Order of Bards Ovates and Druids – www.druidry.org
The British Druid Order – www.druidry.co.uk

Books:

Elements of Druidy – Philip Carr-Gomm
The Art of Conversation with the Genius Loci – Barry Patterson
Druidry: Rekindling the Sacred Fire –Philip Shallcrass & Emma Restall Orr
Druidry – Philip Shallcrass
The Complete Herbal – Nicholas Culpepper
A Druid's Herbal – Ellen Evert Hopman

Made in the USA
Middletown, DE
08 December 2022

17608401R00040